This book belongs to

by Kristin Yu

nǐ hǎo

你好

hello

nǐ hǎo wǒ shì lì li

你好，我是丽丽。

Hello, I'm Lili.

huān yíng lái dào wǒ jiā
欢迎来到我家。

Welcome to my home.

huān yíng

欢迎

welcome

guān xīn

关心

care

wǒ guān xīn wǒ men de huán jìng

我关心我们的环境。

I care about our environment.

wǒ ài hé píng

我爱和平。

I love peace.

hé píng

和平

peace

qǐng

请

please

mā ma qǐng gěi wǒ dú

妈妈，请给我读

yī běn shū hǎo ma

一本书，好吗？

Mum, could you read me a book, please?

tóng qíng

同情

sympathy

wǒ tóng qíng wǒ de péng yǒu

我同情我的朋友。

I sympathized with my friend.

àì

爱

love

bǎo bèi wǒ ài nǐ

宝贝，我爱你。

I love you, baby.

wǒ gǎn ēn
我感恩，
wǒ de mā ma hé bà ba
我的妈妈和爸爸。

I am grateful to my mum and dad.

gǎn ēn
感恩
grateful

xiè xiè

谢谢

thank you

xiè xiè nǐ de bāng zhù

谢谢你的帮助。

Thank you for your help.

bù kè qì de
不客气的。

You are welcome.

you are welcome

duì bù qǐ

对不起

sorry

duì bù qǐ wǒ bǎ bīng qí lín nòng diào le

对不起， 我把冰淇淋弄掉了。

Sorry, I dropped the ice cream.

méi guān xì

没关系

It's okay

méi guān xì xià cì yào xiǎo xīn

没关系，下次要小心。

It's okay, be careful next time.

yuán liàng

原谅

forgive

wǒ cuò le

我错了，

qǐng yuán liàng wǒ

请 原 谅 我。

I was wrong.
Please forgive me.

wǒ ài mā ma de yōng bào

我爱妈妈的拥抱。

I love Mum's hug.

yōng bào

拥抱

hug

fēn xiǎng

分享

share

fēn xiǎng ràng wǒ kuài lè

分享让我快乐。

Sharing makes me happy.

gāo xìng

高兴

happy

bāng zhù wǒ de fù mǔ

帮助我的父母

wèi māo shǐ wǒ gǎn dào gāo xìng

喂猫使我感到高兴。

I am happy to help my parents feed the cat.

yǒu hǎo

友好

wǒ duì rén hěn yǒu hǎo

我对人很友好。

I am kind to people.

kind

wǒ zài nài xīn de děng dài

我在耐心地等待。

I am waiting patiently.

patient

piào liang

漂亮

beautiful

wǒ shì piào liang de

我是漂亮的。

I am beautiful.

wǒ shì wēn róu de

我是温柔的。

I am gentle.

wēn róu

温柔

gentle

chéng shí

诚实

honest

wǒ hěn chéng shí

我很诚实。

I am honest.

wǒ hěn kāi lǎng
我很开朗、
hěn jī jí
很积极。

I am cheerful and positive.

jī jí
积极

positive

juān zèng

捐赠

donate

mā ma xǐ huān

妈妈喜欢

juān zèng wù pǐn

捐赠物品。

Mum loves donating items.

kāng kǎi

慷慨

generous

tā kāng kǎi de jǐ yǔ

她慷慨地给予，

zhī chí tā de péng yǒu

支持她的朋友。

She gives generously to support her friends.

qiáng zhuàng

强壮

wǒ hěn qiáng zhuàng

我很强壮。

I am strong.

strong

wǒ hěn yǒng gǎn

我很勇敢。

I am brave.

yǒng gǎn

勇敢

brave

zhōng chéng

忠诚

loyal

wǒ duì péng yǒu

我对朋友

hěn zhōng chéng

很忠诚。

I am loyal to my friends.

wǒ shì shàn liáng de

我是善良的。

I am kind-hearted.

kind-hearted

xiāng xìn

相信

believe

wǒ xiāng xìn wǒ kě yǐ

我相信我可以。

I believe I can.

wǒ kě yǐ chéng jiù
我可以成就
wěi dà de shì qíng
伟大的事情。

wěi dà
伟大
great

I can achieve great things.

Thank you for purchasing and reading the book. I am grateful and hope you enjoy it. Please consider sharing it with your friends or family and leaving a review online.
Your feedback and support are always appreciated. It allows me to continue doing what I love and providing more bilingual resources for children.

Please follow my book journey @mandarinprodigies

Kristin Yu

Kristin is a native Chinese speaker living in Melbourne, Australia. She is an author of bilingual children's books. Kristin loves to create Chinese resources for children to learn in a fun and engaging way. She is also a mum to three children.

Made in the USA
Middletown, DE
19 September 2023